18 Inspiring Poems
for 11 year olds

Isabella Palladino

Presentation by *BookLeaf Publishing*

Web: www.bookleafpub.com

E-mail: info@bookleafpub.com

ISBN: 9789357441247

First edition 2023

My Favourite Season

I like all the seasons
For different reasons

I like Winter because of the beautiful snow
And I like Spring because of all the things that
grow.

I like Summer because you can have a nice
refreshing dip in the pool
And I like Autumn because it is hot and cool.

But if I was forced to pick one.....

I'd be bound to lose,
Simply because it's impossible to choose!

The Moon

On a star night
When the sky shone bright,
Hiding behind the fluffy clouds,
The moon shone proud.

Up, up in the sky,
Where the little stars lie,
There was the moon, spreading light,
Throughout the dark, gloomy night.

It fills the sky with it's gleaming glow,
But there is one thing that I definitely know,
it's one thing that we can all see,
The Moon, one of Mother Nature's beauty.

The Flower in the Field

There once was a flower in a field,
Hidden behind the grass, it's shield.
But this flower was a special one,
Kept alive by the rain and sun.

The flower was a mixture of purple and blue,
This made it look fresh, this made it look new.
It had a long, green, smooth stem,
It appears that I have found a gem.

As rare and special as it may be,
It's Mother Nature's beauty.
So we shall leave it in peace and not harmed,
And let it sprinkle it's beauty too leave others
charmed. :)

My Special doll

When I was little I had a very special doll,
And I gave it my life, I gave it my soul.
It was my most prize possession,
I took it lessons and all sorts of sessions.

It was with me day and night,
Never did it leave my sight.
I brushed it's hair and sang it songs,
We were together all day long.

But one day, I woke up to see,
My dolly wasn't with me!!
I checked under my bed and on my shelves,
But it must've moved my itself!!

I went to search the whole house,
I scurried round like a mouse.
But I couldn't find her anywhere,
All I knew is that it had to be somewhere.

I sadly stumbled to my room,
All I felt was torture and deep doom.
I put my hand on the door,
And to my surprise I saw.....

My special doll lying on m bed!
My mouth dropped open and I slapped my head.
"Of course" I said.
It must of been under the covers of my bed.

I was relieved and happy to see,
My very special dolly!
I knew I had to keep it safe and sound,
So that we could be together all year round!

Monday to Sunday

Here are the days of the week
A new adventure is what we seek.

First, there is Monday, the start of a new week
and day
There is nothing really left to say.

Then, there is Tuesday, day number two!
Where you can spend it with you, you and you
too!

Next, there is Wednesday,
Where you can sing, dance and play.

Then, there is Thursday, the middle of the week,
When we have fun and little kids squeak.

Next comes Friday, the day of fun,
The day is full of happiness and sun.

Then, there is Saturday, the weekend,
All kids wish that it would never end.

Finally, it's Sunday,
The end of the week, the end of the day.

My Favourite Things

Here are a few of my favourite things.
I love to dance and I love to sing.
I enjoy to bake,
lots of things like cake.

I like to do arts and crafts,
And especially love to giggle and to laugh.
I love to hang out with my friends,
And have sleepovers and let it never end.

I love to eat sweet and sugary stuff,
And play with slime, but not when its rough.
I love all of those things you see,
Because that is what makes me, me!

My Hobbies

I like to do many things.
I like to dance and I like to sing.
I can swim really well,
And the time I can tell.

I am really good at making slime,
In a short amount of time.
I'm really good at making art,
I am finished before I even start.

I'm really good at reading,
And gangs I'm good at leading.
You may wonder how I can do all these things,
You see, That's just how God made me to be.

My little dog

I have a little doggie,
And when he goes outside, he gets rather soppy.
He likes to yap
And he sits on my lap.

He likes to go on walks,
And when he barks, that's how he talks.
He likes to eat treats
Special ones, not like sweets.

His fur is fluffy,
He is very cute puppy.
I will treasure him forever,
And we will be together for ever and ever.

Foods

There are so many different kinds of food,
And you can eat different things, when you are
in a different moods.
There's savoury things and sweet,
And lots of dairy and meat.

There is apples, eggs and cheese,
And frozen things like peas.
There's bread, chocolate and rice,
All of which is very nice.

Then there is ice-creams, sweets and cake,
And lots of things that you can bake.
All of these things taste great,
So how about try them with your mate.

Colours

Colours lighten up our lives,
Bring colours to ourselves, bring colour to
knives,
Bring colours to our clothes, bring colours to
toys,
Bring colour to our world, colour brings joy.

There is pink, green, red,
"That's my favourite colour" lots said.
There's purple, yellow and orange too,
And of course there is blue.

All the colours stand out,
Some scream, some shout!
All used for different things,
But to our world, they all bring bling.

Christmas

Christmas is a special time,
So that's why I thought I write this rhyme,
You eat food, wrap and receive gifts and put up a tree,
And it fills us all with enormous glee.

You eat a massive, warm roast,
And sometimes raise your glass and make a toast.
You pull open crackers and eat the food,
And it always puts you in a good mood.

You wrap presents for your loved ones,
To bring joy, to bring fun.
You also receive gifts to open on the day,
And "Hooray" is all that you can say.

You'll decorate the house all day long,
And do it whilst singing a Christmas song.
Yo decorate a beautiful tree,
And that is why Christmas is important to me!

My Little Sister

I have a little sister called Lili,
Who is rather silly.
She likes to sing and dance,
And compete with me, but I don't give her a
chance.

She likes to go and play outside,
But hates going on big scar rides.
She loves to play with her toys,
And will always brings joy.

She is lots of fun,
And has a bit of gas up her bum!

But still, I love her very much.

Our World

God created this world in a week,
And we are here to seek
Wonderful mysteries every day,
That happen near by, or far away.

Plants begun to grow with fresh, green leaves,
Then God created humans, Adam and Eve.
Animals were also around,
And that brought the Earth lots of sound.

Of course, there is our great big sea,
And so many different kinds of trees.
And that's the world around you and me.

A Brand New Day!

It's the start of a brand new day,
First we'll change, then, we'll play.
Then we shall eat a nice breakfast meal,
Then see how we feel.

Next go outside and do,
Whatever we want too!
And then go and watch something,
then paint anything.

Then we'll sing and dance,
Play a game and give our siblings a chance,
I do so many things that I can't explain,
But tomorrow we will do it all again!

Emotions

Sometimes you are stuck in a certain mood,
Sometimes you are kind, sometimes you are
rude.
Sometimes you don't know how you feel,
Sometimes you don't even believe the way your
acting is real.

Sometimes you are sad,
Sometimes you are glad.
Sometimes you are mad,
And sometimes your are bad.

Sometimes you are happy,
Sometimes you are sappy,
Sometimes we want to be alone,
Sometimes when people ask, we just say "I don't
know"

Dreams

When I dream I fly high,
I reach up, up towards the sky.
I pass the soft, fluffy clouds,
And think to myself aloud.

I land in the world of magic,
Nothing is bad, nothing is tragic.
I skip around and sing,
Because here I can do anything!

I dance and have loads of fun,
Until day is done.
I fly back and wake up from my dream,
Then I sit up and beam.

Roses are red

Roses are red,
Violets are blue,
Everyday I wake up
To a day that is new.

Roses are red,
Violets are blue.
I get out of bed,
And I see you!

Roses are red,
Violets are blue.
I had a normal day,
Like you would do too!

Sleepovers

If you are having a sleepover, here's my advice,
Follow these things, if not, think twice.
Do these things and you'll have a great time with
your friends,
And it will feel like it never ends.

First go out and buy some snacks,
Make sure you have packs and packs.
Next have pizza and watch a movie,
Then have a dance party and get groovy.

Next play truth and dare and have a chat,
Make sure somewhere comfy is where you are
sat.
Have fun till midnight, when you have your
feast,
And make sure you stay up till at least 1am!